THE GRATITUDE ELEMENT

A NEW LOOK AT THE SERENITY PRAYER

Mark T. Scannell

GASSCANN PUBLISHERS
Minneapolis, Minnesota

ISBN 978-0-9966511-0-3 (softcover)
ISBN 978-0-9966511-1-0 (Kindle)

Scripture quotations are from the New Revised Standard Version Bible:
Catholic Edition copyright © 1993 and 1989 by the Division of
Christian Education of the National Council of Churches of Christ in
the USA. Used by permission. All Rights Reserved.

GASSCANN PUBLISHERS

4556 18th Avenue South
Minneapolis, Minnesota 55407
gasscann@bitstream.net
www.thegratitudeelement.com

To my wife Elaine and to the members of my Twelve Step group—very deep thanks yous!

CONTENTS

INTRODUCTION

God, grant me the serenity to accept the things I cannot change,
the courage to change the things I can,
and the wisdom to know the difference.

My premise is that gratitude is an important element of life. Elemental. In this book, I suggest that gratitude, being elemental, should be added to the Serenity Prayer.

This book arose from a happy convergence of two realities in my life: gratitude or giving thanks on the one hand, and a prayer that has been around awhile—the Serenity Prayer, a prayer that is a staple of the addiction recovery movement.

As I have prayed the above rendition of this prayer the past twenty years, additional words and sentiments came to mind. Besides asking for serenity, courage, and wisdom (the core of the prayer), I found myself adding, "I am grateful for the serenity, courage, and wisdom you have given me." Saying these new words along with the words of the old prayer helped me to better express my own gratitude and thanksgiving.

1

Webster's Dictionary describes an element as "one of the constituent parts, principles, or traits of anything; the simplest principles of any system in philosophy, science or art."

Adding the element of gratitude to the Serenity Prayer is a way of closing the loop in the prayer where the emphasis has been on asking. Now there is also thanksgiving for what we have received. Gratitude is not only an important element in living one's life, it is an important additional element of the Serenity Prayer

While exploring the evolution of the Serenity Prayer and the different renditions over the years, I also found that I am not the first person who has suggested a different expression of this prayer. Many have spoken and written about this topic. Their findings further attest to the very positive value and power of gratitude. German mystic Meister Eckhart said, "If the only prayer you ever say in your entire life is 'thank you,' it will be enough."

As I searched through the work and research by many thinkers, the person whose views emerged most powerfully around gratitude was a psychology professor at the University of California-Davis, Robert Emmons. He has done more than talk about the value of gratitude; his extensive research verifies and validates what others have said before and since. He provides many examples from groups he led while trying to gauge the impact of gratitude. Experiment after experiment testified that people who express their gratefulness are happier people. His work has strongly influenced my own thoughts about gratitude.

I focus on a number of points in this book. I devote a chapter on what I believe are important aspects of prayer. I offer my insights into gratitude to point out familiar obstacles to expressing gratefulness, and I suggest practices that can be helpful in coming to live a more grateful life. From there, I look at the main elements of the Serenity Prayer—God/Higher Power, change, serenity, courage, and wisdom, and view these especially in the context of gratitude.

~

Whenever I read a book (and I am an avid reader), I like to know a few details about the author's life, to gain a sense of what may have influenced the writer. Knowing that different perspectives grow out of different backgrounds and experiences, I will tell you a few of mine that influenced what I share in this book.

I grew up as a Roman Catholic in a suburb of Chicago in the 1940s and '50s. After two years of college, I decided to enter a religious community, the Dominicans, and began studying for the priesthood. During the next six years, I studied traditional philosophy and more modern theology, while massive changes were taking place in the Roman Catholic Church. Long-held traditions changed very quickly. For example, the language used in the Mass changed from Latin to the spoken language in each country. In the US, we switched from Latin to English. Some Catholics felt at sea, uncomfortable with these and other changes. But I felt very comfortable. I was ordained a priest in 1969 and served as a priest for the next fifteen years.

In 1984, I decided to leave the Dominican community, in part because I met a woman with whom I fell in love. Elaine and I married in 1985, and we have been married ever since. When I left the religious community, a friend of mine who had a plumbing supply business hired me as manager. Even though I knew very little about plumbing, I had an idea of how to manage a business. I worked there for about twelve years before retiring in 2007.

Throughout my life, I have dealt with various addictions: compulsiveness in thinking and behavior, codependency, and poor boundaries, to name a few. As I have tried to deal with these addictions, I found the wisdom and power of Twelve Step groups, which is where I was first introduced to the Serenity Prayer.

I am deeply interested in promoting and facilitating learning, and it is my conviction that the best learning takes place in community and through dialogue. Learning is not only about discovering what we did not know before; learning also includes discovering and reaffirming what we already know.

To facilitate a sense of dialogue as you read these pages, I have ended each chapter with reflection questions. I encourage you to reflect upon these questions and share your reflections in communities to which you belong. Throughout the book, I include practices designed to integrate gratitude with other aspects of the Serenity Prayer.

My rendition of the Serenity Prayer, which is the focus of these explorations, goes like this:

God/Higher Power, grant me the serenity to accept the things I cannot change;
The courage to change the things I can;
And the wisdom to know the difference.
I am grateful for the serenity, courage, and wisdom you have given me.

I thank you for your willingness to examine whether gratitude is "elemental" in the Serenity Prayer.

CHAPTER 1
Prayer and Praying

Although volumes have been written on prayer by many wise people over the centuries, my intention is to say a few simple things about praying and prayer that will hopefully serve as a foundation and common ground from which to talk about the Serenity Prayer.

Raised in a Roman Catholic religious tradition, I grew up memorizing answers to questions that were created by others. Questions and answers were handed to us in a Catechism of the Catholic Church. There was little room for questions not included in the pages of the Catechism. Questions such as, "Who made us?" or "Why are we here?" were bandied about, and always the "right" answer had to be given. Correct answers (meaning the ones in the book) were rewarded. Wrong answers or other questions were frowned upon by the priests and the nuns who were my classroom teachers when I was growing up.

The same approach was basically true about prayers and praying. We were provided with prayers to recite and memorize so we could say them in whatever situation where a prayer was needed. The Our Father, Hail Mary, and Rosary are examples of this form of prayer.

In the 1960s and '70s, the Roman Catholic Church made a shift away from complete emphasis on memorizing questions, answers, and prayers. Catholics began to think "outside the box"—raise new questions and struggle with some of the teachings of the Church, such as the use of birth control methods. People began to experiment with more spontaneous prayer, even choosing their own words.

During this time, I experienced more poignancy by praying spontaneously than by simply repeating the same traditional prayers. I eventually came to see that there were appropriate times for more traditional types of prayer, as well as for more spontaneous expressions. I well remember folks who were comfortable with this kind of spontaneity, while others definitely were not. Some folks became very uncomfortable when there wasn't an exact prayer to say, and space was left for more spontaneous expressions. Yet others could say a prayer at the drop of a hat and express what they felt deeply at that moment.

Having expressed my preference for more spontaneous forms of prayer, you might find it odd that I was drawn to the Serenity Prayer in the first place—a prayer that has a long history and involves repeating the same words each time. However, even though this prayer has been around quite awhile and said by lots of people, there have been variations in the wording over the years—including the ones I am suggesting.

I began using the traditional wording, and other word choices and sentiments began to enter my mind as I recited this prayer. When words of gratitude began to emerge, I included them naturally. In a way, I enjoyed both forms of prayer, using the traditional words that have been said by many over time, as well as adding my own words. My prayer was old and, at the same time, new. This prayer choice led me to a new expression.

Though I first discovered the Serenity Prayer in the context of a Twelve Step program, using the Twelve Steps does not speak to everyone. There are certainly other paths to help people recover from addictive thinking and behaviors. The Twelve Step path has provided me with a valuable structure for my own recovery. A list of the Twelve Steps is in the Appendix. In providing the list, I chose language that is not exclusionary, such as speaking of God without using male pronouns.

Step 11 of the Twelve Steps talks about prayer and consciousness: "We sought through prayer and meditation to improve our conscious contact with our Higher Power, praying only for the knowledge of whom we are called to be and for the power to carry that out."

This step says simply that prayer and meditation help us develop and maintain a conscious connection to something greater than ourselves. Consciousness is a raised awareness and the intentional seeking of mindfulness. The opposite of consciousness would be lack of awareness, reactive or addictive thinking, or just plain mindlessness.

The Roman Catholic tradition speaks of four different intentions or goals of prayer: petitioning, expressing gratitude, adoring the Godhead or Higher Power, and making amends. Petitioning is simply asking for what we want or need. The Serenity Prayer is largely a prayer of petition, as seen in the words "grant me . . . ," which are used three times.

Prayers of gratitude are about giving thanks for whatever we are grateful for. This prayer intention is missing from the standard version of the Serenity Prayer.

By acknowledging God or a Higher Power, we are giving honor to God or a Higher Power as a form of adoration or worship.

In the tradition of the Twelve Steps, seeking to make amends for what we have done that has hurt others and ourselves is particularly important. Although it is not a formal part of the Serenity Prayer, making amends is a really fundamental part of the 12 Steps, especially Steps 8, 9, and 10 (consult the 12 Steps in the back of this book).

All four of these traditional goals and intentions of prayer provide a good foundation for talking further about how we might pray.

Different traditions suggest ways to develop and maintain consciousness, usually of a Higher Power, while in prayer. We can use words that others have created, as with the Serenity Prayer, the Our Father, or other prayers that have passed on to us over the centuries. We can create prayers for particular situations—such as the death of a friend, the cessation of conflict, or gratitude for a favor received. Other prayer traditions emphasize listening rather than speaking. Such practices are found in Christianity, Zen Buddhism, mindfulness—or centering prayer, prayer of quiet, or contemplation. Many traditions for prayer involve speaking and listening, the same two poles of our conversations with others—including our Higher Power.

Taking this idea a step further—if prayer is both speaking and listening as well as becoming more conscious, then I am open to considering the meaning and purpose of my life and whether I am living consistently in alignment with that purpose.

In using the word alignment, I think of visits to my chiropractor. His adjustments bring me back into physical alignment. Praying, then, is a combination of adjustments and practices we do that bring us back to where we want to be so that we are acting out of what is most important in our emotional and spiritual lives—our values, beliefs, and desires. These "adjustments" are practices a person can pursue individually, as well as being practices that people in communities can pursue together to help achieve and maintain focus and consciousness.

Praying individually gives expression to what is most important to an individual. Such practices include being quiet, expressing our needs, making amends, expressing gratitude, reading spiritual books, and engaging in important conversations with others, including God. The same things take place communally as communities/groups seek to discover what is important, what they value, and what enables individuals to be true to what they believe and hold important.

Buddhist tradition uses the word *sangha* to describe communities of people who come together to support each other in seeking enlightenment. Jesus states (Matthew 18:20), "where two or three are gathered in my name, I am there." A community is any group that is more than one! Two or three are the smallest numbers you can have for a group. Jesus is present in any community gathered together in his name.

Jesus suggests that individuals gathering around a specific goal and/or action experience something larger than themselves. This can be a family, a church, a Twelve Step group, a work group, a support group, or a group coming together to bring about social change. Whether being quiet together, speaking and listening to one another, or even working together, the central focus is about remaining conscious of what the group is doing and trying to do.

For many, it seems that prayer is a means of trying to persuade God or the Higher Power that our way is the way things should be done. I see this often in sporting competitions and academic pursuits: *God, let me or my team win or grant me the "A."*

Telling our Higher Power what we think "should" happen misses the point of prayer. Prayer is not telling God or our Higher Power what should happen. In prayer that seeks to be in alignment with our purpose in life, we ask to be more aware of what God is asking of us. We pray for discernment about the ways in which our Higher Power is speaking to us, and what we are being called to do. This is the core of the adage: "Let go, and let God."

In moments of clarity, I believe that God knows better than I what is best for me, even though I might still struggle with what this is. Praying is trying to learn and discover this and staying connected to the Higher Power in the different ways that this is revealed.

The truth is—prayer helps us be conscious and remain conscious. Prayer helps us stay connected to what gives our lives meaning and purpose.

Reflection Questions

1.) How were you taught to pray (if you were taught to pray), and how do you pray today?

2.) How do you remain conscious and aware today?

3.) What methods, if any, do you practice that keep you aligned individually and/or community?

CHAPTER 2
The Evolution of the Serenity Prayer

So far we have been wading around as though we are in the shallow end of a swimming pool as we have looked at prayer and praying. Now we jump into the deep-water as we consider the known history and evolution of the Serenity Prayer.

In the book *Courage to Change*, author June Bingham told this story about the Serenity Prayer. She ascribed authorship of the prayer to Reinhold Niebuhr in 1934. Niebuhr preached at a church near his home in Heath, Massachusetts. One morning, Howard Chandler Robbins, the dean of the Cathedral of St John the Divine in New York City, was present and asked Niebuhr for a copy of the prayer. Supposedly, Niebuhr said, "Here, take the prayer as I have no further use of it."

Niebuhr wrote a similar comment to Sr M. Bernard Joseph of Mt. St. Mary College, Newburgh, New York, on April 13, 1964. In his letter, Niebuhr stated that Dr Robbins asked for and used the prayer in his monthly report. The prayer was printed on cards and distributed to soldiers during World War II. Alcoholics Anonymous later adopted the prayer, giving it wide circulation.

Other stories suggest that the question of the prayer's authorship is more complex. Loretta Evans, Niebuhr's secretary, said the prayer was not written until 1943. Niebuhr's wife said her husband wrote the prayer during World War II. A summary from Alcoholic Anonymous suggested that an early member of AA discovered the prayer in an obituary in the *New York Times*. He presented the prayer to the AA staff, who saw the prayer as a perfect fit with the principles of AA. The prayer was printed on cards and sent out to members with other literature.

Another possible author of the prayer is a German theologian and mystic, Friedrich Christoph Oetinger. Dr. John E Sasser wrote in an article in *The Grapevine*, the official publication of Alcoholics Anonymous, "while it is not certain that Friedrich Christoph Oetinger (1702–1782) wrote the prayer, it is certain that Reinhold Niebuhr did not write the prayer."

Sasser discovered a building in the mid-1980s in Bergen-Enkheim, Germany, built in 1849, in which the words of the Serenity Prayer were written in German.

Sasser suggests that Oetinger and Reinhold Niebuhr's father were both Lutheran pastors from Germany, and that "Reinhold's father was no doubt familiar with the Serenity Prayer, written by F. C. Oetinger who died 110 years before Reinhold was born."

It is possible that Niebuhr was not aware of hearing this prayer from his father, and that it was part of his spiritual DNA when he composed this prayer for the prayer service described above. This is another way in which prayers are passed on—they are repeated and passed on from generation to generation, and folks are generally not concerned about their source. More important are the feelings and sentiments expressed in the words of the prayer.

~

Let's look at a few different versions of the prayer. Interestingly, the Serenity Prayer has had the same name over the years, with different versions and different authors.

The version of the Serenity Prayer that I grew up with:

God, grant me the serenity
To accept the things I cannot change,
The courage to change the things I can,
And the wisdom to know the difference.

The version, attributed to Friedrich Christoph Oetinger:

God, give me the detachment
To accept those things I cannot alter;
The courage to alter those things
Which I can alter;
And the wisdom to distinguish
One from the other.

Bill W, one of the founders of AA, used the version just quoted in his book, *As Bill Sees It*.

Chester Nimitz, an admiral in the US Navy and commander in chief of the United States Pacific Fleet during World War II, created this next rendition:

God grant me the courage
To change the things I can change,
The serenity to accept those I cannot change,
And the wisdom to know the difference.
But, God, grant me the courage
Not to give up on what I think is right
Even though I think it is hopeless.

Lastly, there is another version attributed to Niebuhr:

God grant me the serenity
To accept the things I cannot change
Courage to change the things I can
And wisdom to know the difference;
Enjoying one moment at a time;
Accepting hardship as the pathway to peace;
Taking, as He did, this sinful world
As it is, not as I would have it;
Trusting that He will make all things right
If I surrender to His will;
That I may be reasonably happy in this life,
And supremely happy with Him forever in the next.
Amen.

The last rendition I found comes from the
Wednesday evening Twelve Step group I have attended for
more than nineteen years. The group has used this version
all during those years, and for many years before I joined:

> God, grant us the serenity
> To accept the things we cannot change,
> The courage to change the things we can,
> And the wisdom to know the difference.

This is the standard version, except for changing the
"I/me" to "we/us." We begin the meeting with the first
person singular and conclude with the first person plural. I
suspect this practice emerged from the group saying this
prayer over time—another example of how living realities
(like prayers) shift as people pray them.

What might we conclude from this short history of
the Serenity Prayer with a name that has remained the
same over these years, though there have been different
renditions and versions?

What this says to me is that any prayer, like the
Serenity Prayer, is a living reality that changes as people

repeat it in prayer over time. Occasionally, prayers disappear, while other change and shift. Regardless of whoever is the original author, we can be reasonably sure that this prayer did not come down from Mt Sinai as Moses brought the Ten Commandments in stone. This prayer flows from person to person and reflects our attempts to put into words our deep feelings about God, and other key components about life.

I believe a Higher Power was at work as different people at different times gave expression to a prayer that clearly had definite similarities to other renditions. There is something Higher Power-ish for this prayer to have continued to be prayed by different groups in different parts of the world for many years. I see the development of this prayer as evolutionary—small changes taking place as people prayed this prayer over time.

I suspect the longer version ascribed to Niebuhr would more likely fit groups that share a particular Christian world view. A shorter prayer is easier for a group to repeat and say than one with many words.

There is a long tradition of a prayer called the "Jesus prayer" in which people repeat a mantra or phrase over and over in silence. One such phrase is: "Lord Jesus Christ, have mercy upon me." This can be a very quieting and relaxing short prayer. Jesus spoke in the sixth chapter of Matthew about not heaping up empty phrases, thinking they will be heard because of their many words (6:7). Jesus says that when you pray, your God/Higher Power knows what you need before you ask (6:8). I conclude from this that there is power in short prayers, whatever is expressed in those prayers. In Buddhist and Zen traditions, the use of a mantra (a word, phrase, or even syllables repeated like a chant) opens the person meditating to a deeper experience.

Reflection Questions

1.) Do you have a favorite prayer or prayers? If you do, what makes a prayer a favorite for you?

2.) Do you feel more comfortable saying prayers others have created? Or do you prefer creating your own prayers?

3.) What prayers have you created? And when?

4.) What do you think about the changes over the years in regard to differences in the Serenity Prayer?

CHAPTER 3
Gratitude

I Am Grateful for the Serenity, Courage, and Wisdom You Have Given Me

I decided to add gratitude to the Serenity Prayer, rather than change the name of the prayer. In doing this, I see myself as following the tradition of people, as outlined in the previous chapter, who at different times added their sentiments and thoughts to this prayer and created different versions of the prayer.

Though I have been praying this prayer for twenty years, I found myself adding to the basics of the Serenity Prayer only a few years ago. This was a kind of synchronistic experience—it came to me by chance, which fits with my belief that prayers are living realities that evolve as people add new ideas and sentiments to their prayers. Change is really a sign of life! I experimented with other words as I continued to pray the Serenity Prayer by being aware of synchronicity and discerning about when to ask for help and when to act on my own. None of the other words resonated the way the word gratitude did.

In my search for other writings and thoughts about gratitude, I discovered Robert Emmons, a professor of psychology at the University of California-Davis, who wrote two books on gratitude: *Thanks: How Practicing Gratitude Can Make You Happier* and *Gratitude Works: A 21-Day Program for Creating Emotional Prosperity*. He has done extensive research on the topic of gratitude. He has written about the research he has done working with many different groups to gauge the effects of expressing gratitude. His work has helped me to see that gratitude is more than a feeling; it is more an attitude that can be developed through repeated expressions of gratefulness.

This story from the New Testament raises another dimension to gratitude that often lies hidden in discussing the topic. The seventeenth chapter of the Gospel of Luke describes the healing of ten lepers.

~

On the way to Jerusalem, Jesus was going through the region between Samaria and Galilee. As Jesus entered a village, ten lepers approached him. Keeping their distance, they called out, saying "Jesus, Master, have mercy on us."

When Jesus saw them, he said to them, "Go and show yourselves to the priests." And as they went, they were made clean. Then, one of them, when he saw that he was healed, turned back, praising God with a loud voice. He prostrated himself at Jesus' feet and thanked him. And he was a Samaritan. Then Jesus asked, "Were not ten made clean? But the other nine, where are they? Were none of them found to return and give praise to God except this foreigner?" Then he said to him, "Get up and go on your way; your faith has made you well."

~

There are a few subplots in this story. Samaritans were foreigners, and people of Jesus' time avoided them because they were thought of as unclean. The people in the story had leprosy, which meant they lived on the fringe of everyday life in their communities. When these unclean foreigners approached Jesus and asked for healing, Jesus did not shy away from them because they were unclean or different. He simply healed them. Only one of the ten healed returned to express thanks.

The story struck me as one of the few times that I noticed Jesus appearing to be keeping score: Weren't there

ten? Where are the other nine? Jesus commends this person
for returning to give thanks and assures him that his faith
and returning to give thanks made him well. All ten were
healed from their leprosy. I do not think Jesus un-healed
the other nine who did not return. Jesus seemed to point to
a deeper level of healing, beyond the physical, for the
person who returned and thanked him.

This story suggests to me that deeper levels of healing
can come about by giving thanks to another. This deeper
healing that comes from expressing gratefulness is the
ability to experience connection, a shift away from isolation
and toward peace and wholeness.

I see gratitude as the opposite of two deeply
destructive feelings that often reside within those of us who
struggle with addiction and compulsivity. The first is
carrying resentments and regrets. Continuing to hold onto
experiences from the past, even when they are long past,
leads us to feel defeated, angry, and overwhelmed, and
concluding that life—especially "my" life—is just not fair.
Have you heard yourself say words like "I didn't get an 'A'
or the degree because the teacher or the department was
unfair. I was unjustly fired, and I have always had to

struggle to find work because of this."? If we are looking for reasons to feel resentment, most of us have many opportunities to feel deeply resentful.

The second deeply destructive feeling is one of entitlement. I deserve special treatment because I am special! I am certainly not like the rest of humanity. Don't you realize who you are dealing with? I deserve added perks because of my pedigree, or I deserve the raise or the bonus just because I am who I am. I deserve another drink because I have worked so hard and deserve special privileges. In feeling entitled, feelings of grandiosity make it difficult to be a regular human being and not expect special treatment. Expressing gratitude is an alternative to both resentments and feeling of entitlement.

Okay, life hasn't always been fair, and different things have happened to me. Am I willing to find reasons for giving thanks anyway? Expressing thanks to others can help me see that I depend on others, and that my life doesn't just revolve around my whims and desires. Others have been instrumental in helping me reach the places I have come in my life. I begin to see how I am really dependent on others.

Scientific studies done by Robert Emmons and his colleagues show that when people regularly engage in cultivating gratitude, they experience multiple benefits—psychologically, physically and interpersonally. Keeping gratitude journals and being specific for what we are grateful for in thanking others are ways to cultivate gratitude.

Emmons describes two dimensions to the expression of gratitude. The first is what he calls recognition. Gratitude is much than a feeling or an expression of politeness. Gratitude is grasping that we are recipients of goodness and gifts from others. Okay, we might have been mistreated or betrayed by others along the way, but there have also been people who have shared their goodness with us. We do not deny our life experience; rather, we are challenged to look for those situations in life when people have gifted us, and say thank you. From my experience, it is difficult to hold onto resentments and regrets while expressing gratitude.

Acknowledging that he had been gifted is what the lone healed leper did who returned to Jesus to acknowledge that he was healed, and to say thank you. There is a difference between becoming aware and acknowledging. In acknowledging, we take another step to say thank you, to show gratitude to the one who has gifted us. Emmons suggests that a major obstacle in expressing gratitude—and I think this is especially true of men in our culture, of whom I am one—is that this manifests as feeling dependent. Who wants to be dependent in a society which so prizes independence and autonomy, not only for men but also for women?

Emmons points out that there is an element of memory involved in showing gratitude. He says in *Gratitude Works!*, "Gratitude is about remembering. If there is a crisis of gratitude in contemporary life, as some have claimed, it is because we are collectively forgetful."

To feel and show gratitude demands that we remember, and we often take things for granted and lose perspective about what we have been given by others. Cultivating gratitude is a commitment not to take life for granted, to recognize what we have been given, acknowledge our thanks to others, and remember.

Jean Baptiste Massieu, a pioneer in deaf education in France, said, "Gratitude is the memory of the heart."

Gratitude, then, involves remembering those who have gifted us and those who continue to gift us; gratitude involves our minds and our awareness of life through the lens of gratitude. Gratitude involves our hearts as we respond emotionally to those who have gifted us and become the beneficiaries of our thanks.

Gratitude is more than a feeling; it is a commitment to act and express thanks to others. Gratitude is a habit at the heart of a person's character—that is developed through repeated actions. I cannot only ask for this habit; I need also to act in grateful ways. I must replace ungratefulness in my life by deciding and choosing to be grateful. Choice and decision are important dimensions to developing habits. Habits do not change overnight. If a habit is deep-seated—like drinking and other compulsive behaviors—it will probably take longer and may involve going back to past behavior in the form of relapses. However long it takes to change a habit, it is important that we begin now. There are no quick fixes to changing habits, especially habits that have been with us a long time.

I have incorporated gratitude in my life in several ways. The first is becoming concrete and specific about how I express gratitude to others. I have found myself being very specific about the times that I have experienced serenity, courage, and wisdom, as well. In the context of the Serenity Prayer, I express this gratitude and thankfulness to my Higher Power. I also thank people who have helped me experience serenity in specific situations. I've thanked people who have helped me take courageous steps in my life and felt grateful to people who have shared their wisdom with me.

A second practice that I have developed is done as I officiate at weddings. When I come home after performing a wedding, I write to the newly married couple and thank them for inviting me to officiate at their wedding and being part of their lives. Though I rarely ever hear from the couples, I am further convinced of the value of expressing my thanks as an important part of my own spiritual practices. Gratitude is really about me, not the other or others. It is really important for me—pure and simple—to give thanks and this is one way I do it.

The third practice of gratitude I have incorporated involves an incident that took place during an argument with a colleague over the phone. I felt broadsided by a letter he sent to someone else without informing me. As we discussed the issue, I felt stung by this man's judgments about me. He said I am the most impatient person he has ever met, that everything I do is ultimately about me needing recognition, and that I am most difficult to work with.

I was angry during the conversation, and I really tried to listen to him. After we hung up, I composed an email to him and apologized for my impatience and thanked him for his feedback. I felt sincere about what I wrote, though I was still upset about his assessment of me. He responded to my email with his appreciation for my listening. I believe that a shift occurred in each of us when I expressed gratitude to him. I found reasons to express gratitude, which did not eliminate my anger, and created a shift in our relationship that has allowed us to continue to work together. I believe this expression of gratitude on both of our parts has allowed us to work together through the rest of our tenure in the organization.

A fourth example of a gratitude practices I have adopted occurs in the context of sharing these ideas with others—both individuals and groups. One fellow reported that he and his wife had begun to add gratitude to their reciting of the serenity prayer each evening. Another woman told me that the priest who prepared them for marriage fifteen years ago strongly encouraged that every evening before they go to sleep, they name five things they are grateful for and one of the five is their partner. This couple has been doing this for more than fifteen years, and the wife said she believes that this is an important part of their strong marriage relationship. Even before I heard this story, I suggested a similar practice to my wife that we do each evening. We try to do it more often than we don't.

More and more, gratitude strikes me as a two-way street—there is saying thanks, and there is receiving thanks, and there is expressing that we have heard the thanks. As I have shared these ideas about gratitude, I have talked about how we typically respond to another's "thank you." The dialogue of "thank you" and "you're welcome" can become rote as we say it so many times. We may say or hear phrases like "it was nothing" or "no problem." Those responses tend to minimize the expressions of gratitude. We need to experiment with new ways of responding to those who express gratitude to us. One of the phrases that has come to me is "I appreciate your thank you (or your gratitude)." If we are going to express gratitude to others, then we need to also be willing to graciously receive the gratitude that others express to us.

German philosopher Martin Heidegger said, "*Denken ist Danken,*" which means to think is to thank. I was intrigued the first time I heard this quote from such a "heady" person like Heidegger. I immediately consulted with a good friend of mine who is a student of Heidegger and asked him for his understanding of the phrase.

My friend suggested that, for Heidegger, thanking was the opposite of controlling things, consuming and using them; it is simply emphasizing the importance of letting things be. Sounds very much like Twelve-Step thinking: simply letting go and letting God! Thanking is the opposite of trying to change and control people, events, and life. How hard that can be at times! Right?

As a Catholic, I am fascinated to see that gratitude is at the heart of the Catholic experience, which is the Mass or the Eucharist. The word Eucharist in Greek means thanksgiving. Without an attitude of gratitude and thanksgiving, the Serenity Prayer is missing a most important and life-giving element!

I now suggest that a life of gratitude is much fuller and richer. I invite you to experiment with the Serenity Prayer adding the line: "I am grateful for the serenity, courage, and wisdom that you have given me."

Reflection Questions

1.) Does your life look any different through a lens of gratitude?

2) To whom are you grateful?

3.) What are the obstacles you feel and experience in expressing gratitude?

4.) How do you receive an expression of gratitude from another person? Do you accept it and take it in, or do you respond with "it's nothing" or "no big deal"?

CHAPTER 4
God, Higher Power, and Synchronicity

My approach to the topic of God combines perspectives
that come from the Twelve Step Recovery movement and
the idea of synchronicity, first mentioned by psychologist
Carl Jung in the mid-1900s. This approach begins with
experience, and ideas emerge as we look at the different
experiences and perspectives.

As I began writing this chapter, a friend gave me a
new book by Thomas Moore, *A Religion of One's Own.*
Moore has written many books about the importance of
caring for the soul—our own individual souls as well as the
soul of the world. In trying to talk about God, Moore
quotes medieval theologian Nicholas of Cusa, who says: "A
theology of unknowing is necessary for a theology of
knowing because without it, God would not be worshipped
as infinite but rather as a creature, and that would be
idolatry."

We humans are prone to making God into our image
and not letting God be God. Nicholas of Cusa is saying
simply that we know more of what God is *not* than what

God *is!* We humans are often tempted to remake God in our own image, instead of seeking to be open to a more expansive God—a God we are unable to control.

A very strong tenet of the Twelve Step Movement is not tying "God" into any single understanding of who that God is. In the Twelve Steps, we hear about "coming to believe in God, however we understand that God." There is no attempt to say this is the only way to understand God or to say this is the God of all churches.

One of my favorite books about recovery is by Ernie Kurtz, *Not God: A History of Alcoholics Anonymous.* Kurtz says that to be in recovery, you don't have to believe in God; rather, you just have to believe that *you are not* God. This realization is absolutely critical in talking about God and a Higher Power. We know very little about God, but one thing that is absolutely critical is that no one of us *is* God. This critical point is a beginning point for recovery from any and all addictions, and any statements we might make about God.

Another piece of the God puzzle comes from the experience of working the Twelve Steps in groups, not just alone. Isolation is a fertile ground for addiction, while the experience of community—however, small or large—is a fertile ground for recovery and sobriety. Jesus speaks of his presence being wherever two or three are gathered in his name. When people gather together in community they are challenged to break out of isolation.

A friend and I attended a retreat on the Twelve Steps a number of years ago at Hazelden, a treatment center in Minnesota. My friend said to the presenter that, at that moment, his Higher Power was the Twelve Step group that he and I attended. The presenter's response was: "That is a good start."

I inwardly cheered at that comment because, at the time, I felt my Higher Power and others' should be God, in keeping with the Judaeo-Christian tradition in which I was raised. I was rather black and white at that point in my life. Looking back on that moment, I would now handle hearing that comment differently. I would argue and disagree because one's Higher Power is what one's Higher Power is, and no one's better than anyone else's.

In his book *True Love* by Thich Nhat Hanh, a Vietnamese Zen Buddhist monk speaks of the need for and importance of "communities of practice" where people can come together and practice ways of loving, speaking, and deep listening—experiences not always part of everyday life these days. A "community of practice" is a perfect way to describe a Twelve Step meeting. Meetings provide support as we try to make changes in our everyday lives.

I now take a more pragmatic approach to the Higher Power. The key is whether one's understanding of a Higher Power works for the person. It might be the God of the Judaeo-Christian tradition or the Higher Power of another spiritual tradition; it might be the group or a community that one belongs to; it might be a value like truth or honesty; it might be one's sponsor. More than anything else, it is not me! We are not our own Higher Power!

In looking at this concept of God and Higher Power—especially as this relates to praying—I suggest that it is possible to view conversation as praying. The often-asked question is: How do I know God hears me, or am I just speaking and hoping, but no one is there to listen?

Another way to posit this question: Does God/Higher Power hear my prayers? I believe God/Higher Power does hear prayers, and that prayer is about our moving into deeper alignment with our purpose. Prayer helps us stay in alignment with God's purpose for us. This can happen even in a community or in conversation with another around significant issues and questions. This is in keeping with what Jesus said about being present when two or three are gathered. Jesus—or one's Higher Power—is there in the exchanges that take place between people speaking and listening.

A story that illustrates this is about a fellow who is trapped on the roof of his house during an extreme flood. He cries out to God for help. Just as he is asking for God's help, a man in a boat comes by and offers to help the stranded fellow. But he says no—he is waiting for God to come and save him. A helicopter comes by, and again the fellow is offered a rescue option. But he again refuses the help, because he is still waiting for God to rescue him. Eventually the fellow drowns. When he meets God, this fellow is angry. He says he asked for God's help and God didn't come to help! God answers, "I sent you a boat and a helicopter, and you said no. What more did you want?"

This story reveals a very important truth—life is not just God/Higher Power and me (or God and you). Rather, it is God and me (God and you) plus the many people who move in and out of our lives. God/Higher Power might most directly address me through my wife, a friend, or even a person hostile toward me. The Twelve Steps reflect this truth by talking not only about God, but also about a Higher Power, and possible different understandings people may have of both of these understandings.

A Higher Power can be a being or thing beyond or different from myself—simply, but it is not ME! God and Higher Power always involve the people with whom we rub shoulders and interact, so it is important to be discerning about whatever these people might be revealing about certain aspects of our life's purpose.

Synchronicity is one of the faces I place on God and the Higher Power these days. I was introduced to synchronicity through a gentleman I met in the early 1970s, Ira Progoff. Progoff spent time studying with Jung at the time when Jung was putting together his thinking on this topic. Jung wrote *Synchronicity: An Acausal Connecting Principle* in 1952, and Progoff wrote *Jung, Synchronicity and Human Destiny* in 1975.

Both men basically say that there are no such things as accidents in life. What we might attribute to chance is more likely to be the deepest unfolding of a person's life. Jung posited in his principle of synchronicity that events fall together not just in ways that can be described by cause and effect. An acausal principle in the universe reveals itself in ways that often mystify and go beyond cause and effect. In my experience, we realize these events have this acausal significance only after the fact. We do not necessarily see their full significance at the moment that they take place. Looking back, we see the significance, their meaning.

A short time ago, I was stuck on a freeway on a Friday afternoon that had become a parking lot because of an accident. I became bored and began to look around. I saw a billboard with the words. "Chance is a Beautiful Thing." I was so struck by these words that I didn't even notice what the billboard was advertizing. What we might usually call chance is really at the heart of this idea of synchronicity. This kind of chance or these kinds of "accidents" are a beautiful thing!

Since beginning to think about synchronicity, through my mentor Ira Progoff, I have seen that most of the richest and most powerful experiences in my life have been synchronistic. The first of these took place in 1955.

My sister and I walked to school together each day, and it was quite a lengthy walk. One morning as we neared the school, a priest was standing on the corner, waiting for a ride.

As an altar server, I knew the routine of these priests who came and said the Mass and then were picked up after the Mass. I didn't know this particular person, but we said hello to each other. He saw the ribbons I was wearing on my belt and asked their significance. I said I was in eighth grade and would be graduating, and these ribbons were part of the graduation ritual. He asked where I wanted to attend high school. I said, "Fenwick!"

The first wave of baby boomers doubled the number of eighth graders applying for admission to Fenwick, which meant that many eighth grade graduates would not be able to attend a private Catholic high school. It was not until after I was accepted into that high school, that the priests from the Church we attended told my parents about that priest that I told I wanted to attend Fenwick. Turns out, he was the principal. He had gone back to the rectory the day I met him and asked if there was an eighth grade applicant with my name. They said yes. He told them, "He is accepted—anyone who wants to go to this school with that enthusiasm will be accepted."

I did attend Fenwick and eventually entered the religious community that ran the school. I remained part of that community for twenty-three years. Though I had no idea of any of this in 1955, while walking to school with my sister; years later, I came to consider this meeting and what happened as moments of synchronicity.

Moments of synchronicity do not always have to be high moments or moments of success. As Progoff pointed out, the spiritual journey—the journey for meaning and purpose as well as often the journey toward recovery—is composed of both moments of connection and disconnection. At times, there are moments of disconnection that lead to deeper experiences of connection. Without an often painful disconnection, there would not be a significant moment of connection.

Another moment of synchronicity took place over a period of a year or so around 1969. As I came closer to ordination as a priest, I had decided in consultation with my superiors that a good next step was to attend the University of Minnesota and work toward a doctorate in social psychology. I thought everything was in order and that I would be moving to Minneapolis in August of 1969. One day in July, I received a phone call from the university saying that I was not accepted and shouldn't come due to missing prerequisites. I answered that I thought we had discussed that I needed a few prerequisites, and I thought I could take them when I began. When the answer was no, I felt a dark cloud descending on my life; I didn't know what I would do next at this last hour. I decided to stay in Iowa and begin work toward a doctorate in theology.

In early fall, a good friend of mine who was a priest in the same community—the same Heidegger expert I mentioned earlier—invited me to travel with him. Essentially because I didn't have much to do, I said yes. We spent the weekend with the leadership group of a religious community of women, who were trying to adjust and create with the changes taking place in the Catholic Church in the late 1960s. As a result of this weekend, they invited me to teach in their summer school that summer. Toward the end of the three weeks, I learned that I was going to be invited to lead a retreat in early September for the young members of their community, returning to finish degrees.

However, when I was asked, I declined. I was starting a new job and didn't think I could fit this in. But the woman prevailed. I finally agreed that if two priest friends of mine would come, I would consider doing the retreat. I thought the chances of reaching them in mid-July were next to impossible and, even if I reached them, one or both would say no. To my amazement, I reached both of them on the first calls. Even more to my amazement, they both said yes. So, the three of us showed up to lead this retreat.

The synchronicity of all of this, you ask? During the retreat, I met the woman who later became my wife. I certainly had no idea of this when I was told no by the University of Minnesota, when I went with a friend for a weekend along Lake Michigan, or when I did everything possible to avoid giving this retreat. This un-knowingness at the moment is part of these moments of synchronicity. Only later do we catch sight of their greater significance for our lives and probably the lives of others. And we may also glimpse the face of God or a Higher Power.

I saw an important synchronistic moment in the situation I mentioned earlier about a friend of mine hiring me to work at his company in plumbing, even though I knew little about plumbing. I was closing my counseling practice, feeling shame due to mistakes I made. I began to tell people I was leaving this work and was looking for different work. When I was speaking with Stu, he spoke about his being disappointed by my news. We continued to talk. At one point, he asked whether I knew anyone who might be interested in helping him manage his plumbing business.

I said, "Yes."

He said, "Who?"

I said, "Me!"

He said, "You?"

I said, "Yes!"

That dialogue changed my life. A couple of days later, he hired me. I went on to work for and with him for fifteen years. The shame around my mistakes gave way to feelings of gratitude for what happened and where I ended up. I hurt people by thinking I knew what was best for others, without being open to any feedback or consultation. My arrogance and pride hurt others. Now, I call these events of synchronicity, where a Higher Power was involved in my life, although I only realized it as I looked back. In this case, the Higher Power also included the real people of my life, such as Stu, people I hurt deeply, and others who extended a hand of support and welcome. That is Higher Power! That is God! That is synchronicity!

The challenging aspect of synchronistic moments is that we cannot make them happen. They are not based on cause and effect. They are happenings, and they just show up. So we need to be open to what might be happening.

In my examples, they happened in the midst of everyday experiences. The fellow on the rooftop, who was near drowning and considerably arrogant, did not see the synchronicity of the boat and the helicopter showing up as an answer to his prayers. He wanted God to show up and act! A particularly strong instance of grandiosity!

An important aspect of synchronicity is being willing to be discerning about what is happening in a particular situation and what choice we might make in the here and now. I have come to believe that synchronicity happens the more we are open to it happening. Can you conceive of an acausal principle—complementing cause and effect—that is active and alive in the world? If so, that influences what you see and what you will do.

I have asked the Higher Power to help me be more aware of how synchronicity is working in my life and what I can do to tap into that principle. I have noticed that others can at times help us be more discerning to the synchronicity taking place in our lives. We may be too close to see what is really happening. Showing up for life opens us to the possibility of experiencing synchronicity. There is less chance-for synchronicity when we isolate ourselves and remain disconnected.

A fourteenth century book on meditation, *Cloud of Unknowing*, was written by an anonymous person. Historians have suggested that the author remained anonymous perhaps because his writing about spirituality could have led to his death. The author's theme is that unknowing is way to coming to knowledge. This offers another meaning to the idea of letting go—letting go of what we have learned as a way of becoming in favor of what we do not know.

Being willing to live in an "unknowing" frame of mind is a way to break through the polarization around us in the world. We are challenged to find ways of coming together that move us beyond "I am right and you're wrong." These ways may be found by entering into a cloud of unlearning and learning what we did not know—with God or our Higher Power.

For me, this principle of synchronicity has become the face of God and my Higher Power. There are no accidents. More is happening than any of us can see. There are many different ways to name this mystery. At times we need a community to help us experience a Higher Power; and at other times, we can be profoundly alone and experience God or our Higher Power.

In line with gratitude, let's acknowledge our dependence and our being the recipient of goodness and gifts by giving thanks to a God or Higher Power in prayer. Try experimenting with: "I am grateful to God/Higher Power for the serenity, courage, and wisdom you have given me."

Reflection Questions

1.) Do you believe in God? If so, how did you come to learn about God?

2.) How do you experience God or your Higher Power? Have you gone through times of unknowing and non-belief in God or a Higher Power?

3.) What have moments of synchronicity looked like in your life?

4.) How have you been moved to express gratitude to your Higher Power for different experiences? How have you expressed this?

CHAPTER 5
Change

After speaking about God, Higher Power, and synchronicity, I want to unpack other elements of the Serenity
Prayer. I was struck by the word "change"—accepting the
things I cannot change, courage to change the things I can,
and the wisdom to know the difference. Change is an
important element of this prayer. I did not initially see this;
it only emerged as I spent time praying this prayer and
considered its main elements.

An ancient Greek philosopher, Heraclitus, said
everything in life is changing—no one can step into the
same river twice. Another Greek philosopher, Aristotle,
spoke about change being a sign of life. If there is no
change, there is no life. We certainly live in a time of
accelerated change—what is here and in favor today is gone
and out of favor tomorrow. As a sports' fan, I am struck by
the use of instant replay to make sure the official makes the
right call. The replay slows down the play so that it is easier
to see if the call was the right one. We are able to see the
same play from different angles. We try to slow down the

changes we are experiencing, but nothing seems to work. Change continues to happen!

When I work as an amateur umpire, umpiring softball games in the parks of Minneapolis, there is only one umpire. That means only two eyes judging the plays, not like in the major leagues with four umpires and eight eyes. And we have no instant replay! At times, I sense that the players want the same kind of correct calls that instant replays bring. Plays, at times, happen so quickly, it is difficult to make the right call.

I find myself looking at the Twelve Steps through this perspective of fast changes. People have suggested that recovery—especially for white, middle-class men, from whom the Steps came—is about power and powerlessness. Does this mean that recovery essentially boils down to an attempt to deal with change? I am beginning to think so.

Change is a constant—the seasons of the year, the aging process of each and every one of us, the transitions we are continually going through in the different aspects of our lives. A book that became my bible regarding change is *Transitions: Making Sense of Life's Changes* by William Bridges, first published about twenty-five years ago.

Bridges' insight is that in every transition, there are three stages: the ending, the beginning and—the most important stage—the in-between as we try to make sense about what is happening and where we are going. In the face of change, we are often powerless, possibly feeling out of control and with a deep sense that our lives have become unmanageable. This is at the heart of Step 1. The following Steps, then, are simply ways to respond to these feelings of powerlessness and unmanageability in the face of the change we are experiencing.

In addition to all the outer changes that we are experiencing and see taking place all around us, there is another kind of change taking place, more of an inner change. When discussing with this with a friend of mine, he said that the inner change is a movement from "I" to "we."

In the Judaeo-Christian tradition, we use the Greek word "metanoia" to mean a change in heart. As we shall see later on, the heart is a main focus of the Serenity Prayer. This prayer is not an intellectual exercise or just repeating prayers; rather, it is changing our hearts from turned inward to outward, toward others; and trying to find a balance between independence and dependence. An inner change is necessary to begin to deal with all the outer changes we are experiencing in our lives. Life is dealing with the different transitions we are continually experiencing. The Zen Buddhist tradition uses the word *satori* to describe a flash of sudden awareness that can lead a person to make changes in their life.

As Greek philosophers have told us, change is a given—no change, no life. The choice—and I mean choice—is how we will deal with these changes. Will we drift into hopelessness, despair, and frustration? Or can we find the inner stamina to choose engagement, creativity, and hope?

Bridges believes that the in-between stage is where the possibilities exist for change and re-direction. It is possible that if we do not honor the in-between, we will miss out on the new possibilities that might be emerging. We will just continue to repeat what we have always done. Another part of honoring the in-between is to talk with others and ask for help. There is an old Zen saying that when the student is ready, the teacher will show up. Part of this inner change in our transitions is a readiness and openness to hear the teachers, whoever they might be. There is no inner change without this openness and readiness to listen and learn.

The Twelve Steps begin with an acknowledgment of powerlessness, and this powerlessness can be in any area of our lives. Step One states that we admitted we were powerless over addictive behavior, that our lives had become unmanageable. The movement of the Steps is really about empowering the individual to make changes and choices to move gradually out of this powerlessness. The Twelve Steps help us move from powerlessness to empowerment.

Beginning to feel a sense of empowerment enables a person to choose and to act—regardless of what the situation might be. I have often thought that we need a thirteenth Step—having been empowered by naming our powerlessness, finding ways to surrender to a Higher Power and by finding resources, I am able to continue to work with the other areas of life where there is powerlessness and unmanageability. Because, at times, it is finding the courage to act and make changes; at other times, it is accepting that this is the way things are, and it is time to get on with life.

How we deal with change has enormous impact upon our lives and in staying out of reactive and addictive habits and practices. The Serenity Prayer and the Twelve Steps give us important clues on how to do this.

Reflection Questions

1.) How do you deal with change—hate it? love it? somewhere in between?

2.) What transitions are you going through at the present time, and what do these changes say to you about the movement of your life? Do you feel out of control and powerless?

3.) Looking back at a major transition in your life—how did you deal with the change? What made the transition more challenging? What helped you?

4.) What changes in your life have evoked gratefulness?

CHAPTER 6

The Serenity to Accept
What I Cannot Change

We will now look at the different sentiments expressed in the Serenity Prayer. We will look at what we are asking for, what obstacles prevent these sentiments from becoming part of our lives, and what practices we might pursue to further develop this virtue or attitude. We are asking for a serenity that enables us to accept the things we cannot change. This clear statement acknowledges that there are things in our lives that we cannot change, and we are asking for the serenity to accept these things. In asking for serenity, it is helpful to name what it is we are seeking. This naming or praying centers us and opens us to experience the serenity and peacefulness we are asking and searching for and leads to a deeper sense of gratitude.

Our inability to connect with others is a major obstacle to experiencing serenity. Judgments we make about ourselves and others, and the expectations we carry within ourselves from which we act, can both threaten our desire for serenity. In making judgments about others, about what is important and what is not—we are making comparisons with others.

Comparing ourselves with others is very easy to do as we are continually bombarded by advertising. The media tells us what we should be buying, wearing, and looking like. In essence, the media tells us what should be important in our lives. Trying to "keep up with the Jones" can feel like we are forever on a treadmill. This can create deep feelings of unrest and anxiety. "Oh my God, we don't measure up or look like this very attractive person we see on TV!" Making these judgments about ourselves and others often keeps us un-serene and often in fretful places.

Closely associated with making judgments are the unreasonable expectations we try to meet. So whose expectations are we trying to meet? In a book I read many years ago, *The Lonely Crowd* by David Riesman and Reuel Denney, the authors speak about a change they saw taking place in which behavior was shifting from an inner-directed perspective—a perspective from which behavior arose more from an internal perspective, formed at an early age by parental figures and elders. They saw a new perspective emerging in these more "modern" times in which people were becoming more other directed. In this other-directed focus, people were becoming more attuned to their peers and the cues presented by the media.

Without doubt, they were right sixty-five years ago. The trend to more other-directedness has only increased in these intervening years. We are continually bombarded by messages wherever we are and wherever we look. Access to social media only exacerbates this other-directedness.

Another source of worry and anxiety is carrying resentments toward others. At times, these resentments deal with events that happened many, many years ago. By continuing to carry these resentments, the old events stay alive within us, as though they just happened yesterday.

In the Serenity Prayer, we ask for serenity, yet judgments, other-directedness, and resentments can disturb our serenity and our sense of gratitude. I doubt that anyone is 100 percent serene for very long. I have never felt serene for long periods of time. My hope is that we come to live with less anxiety and worry. The first practice is praying the Serenity Prayer, and asking for serenity, especially when we are feeling anxious and insecure.

A second practice is to develop more gratitude in our lives. A practice I have found helpful is thinking about someone to whom I feel grateful. As I think about such a person and identify reasons for my gratitude, I begin to shift away from feeling so anxious. Emmons in his book *Thanks*, mentioned earlier, offers a number of studies he has conducted that speak of the power of gratitude in restoring serenity. We are unable to remain as anxious if we begin to think of a person for whom we are grateful. Feelings of anxiety and gratitude cannot exist at the same time—and important insight when seeking to experience both serenity and gratitude more deeply.

Gratitude can also help us deal with the resentments. When we carry resentment toward a particular person, we may find healing by looking for a reason to feel grateful for that person. This does not mean that we deny what happened with this person. What it does mean is that we are willing to look for other, better things about this person, and not remain stuck in our resentment. For example, I carried resentment toward a person with whom I worked. As I thought about this person, it struck me that the person has taught me how to be more patient, and I can grateful for this aspect of the person. It works.

The next couple of practices involve engaging our bodies in restoring serenity. The first is simply becoming aware of our breathing and taking deep breaths. Being aware of our breathing connects us with ourselves at a very deep level and helps to ground us in whatever situation we find ourselves. A Psalm in the Hebrew Bible speaks to this (Psalm 46, verse 10): "Be still and know that I am God." We become aware of different perspectives in stillness and quiet that we are not aware of amidst the noise and activities of life. I tend to re-phrase the Psalm as: "Be still; be aware of your breathing, and you will possibly experience a Higher Power and serenity."

Another helpful practice when feeling flooded by strong emotions—perhaps when we remember a very stressful experience or a smell reminds us of a painful memory—is to practice becoming centered. When triggered like this, a method that has helped me is to sit in a chair where I can reach under the seat and pull upward, pressing me more solidly into the chair. This exercise helps me return to my body, and the flooding emotions decrease. This practice helps rekindle serenity.

Another method is to hold onto a physical object as we face an experience that creates anxiety. I have a friend who, when he has to speak to a group he finds threatening, carries a small Gideon Bible. When he speaks, he holds onto the Gideon. I have seen his Bible, and its pages are very tattered and wrinkled, which speak of his using this approach often. This works for him and helps him speak when he feels threatened.

As my friend described this approach, I thought how similar that is to the Roman Catholic tradition with sacraments; an external object, such as oil, water, bread, wine, or a Bible becomes the vehicle of inner change and transformation. It could be that carrying an object in our pocket that, when we touch it, brings about an inner change. Perhaps it is a smooth stone, a coin, or a medal. We move from agitation closer to serenity. A physical object can, thus, become a vehicle for inner quieting.

Feeling anxiety keeps us from being in this present moment. We have slipped into a memory from our past where there was anxiety, or we have moved into the future, trying to deal with fears about things that have not happened. Simply breathing helps us return to the present moment in our lives. Returning to present time can help us find serenity again.

With different practices, we are seeking to move toward an acceptance of certain things in our lives that we cannot change. I can't change I am seventy-two years old as I write this; I am not in control of everything in my life as I live in a world in which others are making choices that lead to results over which I have no control or minimal control at best. The only thing I can do is really surrender—not in a kind of passive giving in; rather, this is the way things are, and I choose to accept that this is the way things are.

These practices can enable us to live with more serenity as well as gratitude. The more I am able to accept my life with its ups and downs and successes and failures, the more I will experience greater serenity and develop a stronger habit of gratitude.

Reflection Questions
1.) Are there realities in your life that you cannot change, which lead you to feel worried, powerless, and anxious? What do you usually do in these situations?

2.) What have you found helpful in regaining your serenity?

3.) Is there someone toward whom you feel resentment? Is there anything you can feel grateful for in relation to this person?

4.) What moments of serenity stand out especially in your life? Did you ever express gratefulness concerning any of those experiences? If you did, to whom or how did you express your gratitude?

CHAPTER 7
The Courage to Change the Things I Can

Having dealt with the things we can't change for which we ask for serenity, we come to the courage to change the things we can. The opposite of courage is fear. What first comes to mind are the immortal words of Franklin Roosevelt during World War II that we have nothing to fear but fear itself. By stating what we fear—I fear losing my job, I fear missing the plane—we concretize our anxiety, lessoning its hold on us. It is this specific thing—not everything. Naming what we fear is a major step toward addressing what it is and choosing to do something about it. Making choices to do something about what we fear can also make us more aware of our gratefulness; we can be grateful for the choices we made and the people who supported us.

This part of the Serenity Prayer specifically states the conviction that there are things we can do about our fears or our inaction; we can make changes and we can act. We do not have to remain in a powerless place forever. We do not have to remain forever mired in Step 1, feeling powerless as well as feeling that our lives have become unmanageable.

Being a wordsmith, I am struck by the word courage stemming from a French word *cour*, meaning heart. From its French roots, then, courage is about an energy that arises from the heart. It is not primarily a rational or intellectual experience. We are talking more about an energy rather than thoughts or ideas. If you watch a horse leap over a fence, the horse leads with its heart. The heart goes over first. That is a powerful image for me to describe the energy of courage. Our heart—our courage—leads us over the fence to face what scares us, and enables us to act.

The Serenity Prayer acknowledged already that there are things that are out of our control, over which we are powerless. Here the prayer speaks of there being things over which we have control and we can make changes. We do not have to remain in a powerless place. When I am in a situation that I feel is unfair or unjust, I can speak out as well as act to make a change. I can volunteer for a project that can change what is happening, I can become active in a political cause, I can bring meals to people who are shut in, or I can become involved in a neighborhood or civic event.

A professor of mine years ago spoke about the paralysis of analysis. It is so easy to get stuck in *thinking* about or in analyzing situations that we never *act*. We get trapped in procrastinating about what to do. There is an intimate link between procrastination and perfectionism. Often we are afraid to act for fear of making a mistake. Rather than risk making a mistake, we do nothing. For many of us, it is perfectionism that is part of our addiction. We start thinking or acting addictively to medicate feelings related to both procrastination and perfectionism. This part of the prayer, then, is about asking for the courage to act— to make the changes we think need to be made, even if we might be wrong. That is the risk, because a courageous act is not a protection from making mistakes. On the other hand, nothing ventured, nothing gained.

To exercise courage, it is helpful to be part of a community that can support us with changes we want to make. This is both in regard to changes in our individual lives—like taking steps to work less, drink less alcohol, trying to live a more balanced life—or changes that involve the larger societies to which we are belong. A woman I know decided to run for the school board in her community because she believed certain aspects of the educational system were missing. I know people who regularly bring meals to parts of their community where people are lacking food. I know people who volunteer, stepping out of their comfort system, to read in schools, helping young people learn to read.

In the last year, I have been exposed to research that is being done on the development of our brains. I owe my education here to two women, Ann Betz and Ursula Pottinga, who have begun a series of courses under the umbrella they call BEabove Leadership. They explore the field of neuroscience as it relates specifically to the field of life coaching. They have developed a schema for helping people move from what they describe as living "below the line"—hopelessness, fear, and frustration—to living "above the line"—engagement, innovation, and synchronicity. To learn more about this system, visit their website: Beaboveleadership.com.

In regard to this aspect of the Serenity Prayer, these women suggest that what enables a person to move from "below" to "above" is courage. It takes courage to move from fear and frustration to connecting and creating. Another fascinating dimension in this regard is the development of new neuropathways in our brains. As we act and do the same thing over and over, we are literally developing pathways in our brains—like creating ruts. That is why it is often difficult to do something new, especially when it involves trying to change a habit we have done the same way for a long time. An old saying speaks to this: it is hard to teach old dogs new tricks. But you *can* learn new tricks by developing new pathways in the brain. We are never too old to learn "new tricks." But we won't learn new tricks if we believe we can't and we continue to do what we have always done! We can begin, for example, by eating healthier food and doing some exercise.

This neuroscience explanation explains why it is so difficult to change behaviors that we have become habituated to. This is certainly the case with addictive behaviors practiced over a number of years. We cannot just change them in the wink of an eye. We need courage to change, to begin to behave differently as well as reach out for the support to keep doing this new behavior. As we develop new habits, we develop new pathways in our brains.

Emmons in *Thanks* suggests that it takes twenty-one days to change a habit. We need to do the same thing for twenty-one consecutive times to begin to dislodge an old way of acting and develop a new pathway in our brains. It may be hard to believe that a deep-seated habit, like an addiction, can be changed that easily. Emmons is saying that habits *can* change and it takes repeated actions day after day for a new habit to form. The change might take twenty-one days, or it might take ninety. What is important is that we take the first step to begin.

In my own experience, setting a goal helps me to begin to make a change. Years ago when I was a runner, I read an article that recommended setting a manageable goal when you first start running. The author suggested a simple activity, like putting on one's shoes for the first few days. Then add walking around the block daily for a week. Each week do more, and as you experience success, go further, push harder. This same idea fits with finding the courage to make any change. Start small, build toward larger changes by successfully accomplishing the smaller steps. This approach has-shown to release dopamine in the brain, which helps us feel good. As we reach each goal, there is new energy and the possibility of feeling like I can take on other, better habits in my life that might have seemed too hard before. Momentum can begin to build and grow.

Making changes this way also involves having the courage to act differently, a willingness to be accountable for completing our goals, and asking for support in making this kind of change. This book is an example of this method for me. I had tried to write this book for a long time. But I finally shared this secret goal with others. I said what I was going to do, and I asked people for support and feedback. I even invited these people to ask me how the book was coming from time to time. I hired an editor to help me be clear about my message. I engaged helpers with the production of the book as well. I was trying to do something I had never done, and this required the courage to break the habits that stymied me in the past. The very fact that you are reading this book is evidence that I was able to create new pathways in my brain. I behaved differently with the support of others all along the way.

This also led me to become more aware of those people who helped me act more courageously while writing this book and my deep feelings of gratitude for them were tapped. It is possible for an old dog to learn new tricks with a little help from one's friends!

As the first part of the Serenity Prayer speaks about learning to accept what we cannot change to find serenity, the second part, having the courage to change the things we can change, invites us to take risks and courageously try to change even when the idea of change may cause us as feeling of unrest, not a feeling of serenity. This is the paradox—as we seek serenity, we move toward and then through agitation. This leads to the next part of the Serenity Prayer: asking for the wisdom to decide which is the path that is appropriate here and now?

ESPN sports' personality Stuart Scott wrote, in his book *Every Day I Fight,* about his battle with a very rare form of cancer. He had many procedures and spent many days in the hospital before losing his fight in January 2015.

At one point he spoke about the value of having the courage to admit that he was afraid. Admitting fear is being courageous. When we courageously admit openly to another how we are truly feeling when anxious or afraid, the thing we fear may still be there, but we have taken the first step in speaking truth and behaving with courage. This is always a good thing, even if it might be difficult. In his show of courage, Stuart Scott has become a hero to me by showing courage in a very difficult situation. If he can do that, why can't you or I?

I have learned again and again that it is difficult to be courageous alone, especially when I am facing, or trying to change, something that feels truly monumental. A community can be crucial in helping to figure out what to do and following through with actions that seem right. From this perspective within a community, I can begin to identify people to whom I am truly grateful for their support and encouragement. Courage and gratitude are often two sides of the same coin in trying to make changes and in finding the courage to step out and take a risk.

Reflection Questions

1.) What absolutely scares you? What have you tried to do with this situation?

2.) Where have you acted courageously in your life? Did you express gratitude for these moments of courage?

3.) What habit here and now do you want to change? And what are you willing to do to take this plan of action? How will you begin, and who can you ask for support?

4.) On a continuum from hopelessness to synchronicity, where do you most often find yourself? Below the line? Above the line?

CHAPTER 8
The Wisdom to Know the Difference

Wisdom can be the most difficult perspective of the Serenity Prayer to understand and comprehend. This aspect takes the plea for serenity and the asking for courage and raises the question of which to pursue at any one moment in time. How do we discern the difference between either in a particular situation? And what is wisdom?

I begin with two stories from antiquity. The first comes from the Hebrew Bible—from the First Book of Kings, chapter 3, verses 5–12.

At Gibeon the Lord appeared to Solomon in a dream by night; and God said, "Ask what I should give you." And Solomon said, "You have shown great and steadfast love to your servant David, because he walked before you in faithfulness, in righteousness and in uprightness of heart toward you; and you have kept for him this great and steadfast love, and have given him a son to sit on his throne today. You have made your servant your king, although I am only a child; I do not know how to go out or come in.

And your servant is in the midst of the people you have chosen, a great people, so numerous they cannot be numbered or counted. Give your servant an understanding mind to govern your people, able to discern between good and evil . . ." It pleased the Lord that Solomon had asked this. God said to him, "Because you have asked this, and have not asked for yourself long life or riches, or for the life of your enemies, but have asked for yourself understanding to discern what is right . . . Indeed I give you a wise and discerning mind."

The dialogue between Solomon—traditionally a figure of wisdom in the Bible—and the Lord/Higher Power—strikes at the heart of the Serenity Prayer. Solomon speaks to God from his experience of powerlessness, of feeling overwhelmed by the role he has chosen to play. When asked by his Higher Power what he seeks, he asks for an understanding and discerning mind that will help him discern between good and evil. He is rewarded by the Lord for what he asked for, and not riches or the vanquishing of his enemies. Isn't this what we are seeking as we pray this part of the Serenity Prayer? Isn't this really the ability really to discern between accepting what is and choosing to act to change things?

The second story goes back to the Greek philosopher Plato. Through his mouthpiece, Socrates, he speaks about wisdom in the *Dialogue with Theaetetus*. In the dialogue, there is mention that both philosophy and wisdom begin in wonder. Traditionally, there is a sense that wisdom is only the prerogative of the old, and rests upon how much a person knows. The wise person knows a lot, and in our society probably has multiple degrees that show the person knows a lot.

But there is a vast difference between knowledge and wisdom. Libraries are filled with lots of books of what learned people have said and think. Wisdom is very different. Wisdom is the fruit of life experience. Wisdom emerges out of reflecting and learning from a person's and other peoples' life experiences.

From Plato, a key ingredient of wisdom is developing a healthy sense of wonder. The wise person has developed a strong sense of curiosity. In the words of George Bernard Shaw from *Back to Methuselah*, Act 1, "You see things and you say 'Why?' But I dream things that never were; and I say 'Why not?'" That is curiosity; that is wondering about what hasn't happened yet or wondering what the meaning is of what happened. Asking for a discerning mind and heart helps us to know the difference, and decide what to do here and now in our lives.

These qualities of wonder and curiosity are often lost as we age, attend school, and acquire degrees. Wonder and curiosity can tap gratefulness within us as see realities we had not seen before. Gaining knowledge often replaces curiosity and wonder. For a long time, I have been struck by another New Testament passage where Jesus says: "Unless you change and become like a child, you will never enter the kingdom of heaven." (Matthew 18:3) I equate childlikeness with the qualities of wonder and curiosity, and in this passage, Jesus connects becoming like a child with a different way of perceiving reality—a perception he connects with seeing things that not everyone sees.

Developing wisdom means continuing to stay curious and continuing to wonder. From this perspective, wonder and curiosity are more important in seeking wisdom than being able to give correct answer after correct answer on examinations. Degrees are not true indicators of wisdom; the ability to be curious is.

Another interesting dimension in the Solomon story is that the encounter between Solomon and the Lord takes place at night. That possibly reveals another perspective about wisdom, that wisdom might not always be in the realm of the conscious—the stuff of daylight. There is also the realm of the unconscious that speaks in the dark and at night. How many of us have had experiences in dreams that have caused a shift in consciousness? Or revealed a different path to take?

Similar to the chapter on God and synchronicity, there are times when we become aware only after about how significant a meeting was, and how that meeting reshaped our life. Moments of synchronicity are often like waking-dreams. We are awake, yet things are happening that are leading us in different ways. Both night dreams and these moments of synchronicity provide wisdom, giving us other ways to look at our lives.

I am more aware of these waking dreams and their impact upon my life. I know numerous others who have very rich dreams that they use to discern where their life is taking them. Both can be the source of wisdom that this aspect of the Serenity Prayer is pointing toward, and they can awaken gratitude within us as we see where and how we have been led as events unfolded.

The "knowing" of knowing the difference is much, much more than just reading books, going to classes, and listening to talks and lectures. This is part of wisdom, and yet the wisdom of the Serenity Prayer is also much, much more. The best word that I have come up to describe this way of knowing, is that it is more intuitive; it is a way of knowing that might defy what we expect. For me, it seems to come out of nowhere.

What has helped me in trying to become more intuitive is listening. Listening is especially critical—a listening that is both of oneself as well as others. This seems even more important in an environment with so much noise and clatter.

"What am I aware of here and now?" This question fits with developing a sense of mindfulness, of being aware of what is happening both within us and all around us. Taking time to just simply breathe is grounding and helps me more mindful of what is happening. This brings me back to Plato: "An unexamined life is not worth living." Being mindful is another way of examining our lives.

Discern might be a better word than "to know the difference." Discerning has a quality of pondering, of discovering an awareness. One of the meanings from *The Random House College Dictionary* is "to distinguish or discriminate."

Wisdom is often a struggle to know what to do here and now. This is a kind of knowing that involves trying to figure out what to do in the face of two options, which both seem good. This calls for a deeper kind of knowing, a discernment, and often involves seeking the feedback and insight that comes not only from others but also from our deeper selves.

Other ways to facilitate this intuitive way of knowing are letting go of negative feelings and thoughts, and developing a deep sense of connection with all of life. I have been struck by the work of Brene Brown on shame and the impact of shame on our lives. The title of her book *Daring Greatly* was inspired by part of a speech that Franklin Roosevelt gave many years ago. (The solely male references in this speech are indicative of the time in which the speech was given by Roosevelt.)

~

It is not the critic who counts; not the man who points out how the strong man stumbles, or where the doer of deeds could have done better. The credit belongs to the man who is actually in the arena, whose face is marred by dust and sweat and blood; who strives valiantly; who errs; who comes up short again and again; because there is no effort without error and shortcoming; but who actually strives to do the deeds; who knows great enthusiasms, the great devotions; who spends himself in a worthy cause; who at best knows in the end the triumph of high achievement, and who at the worst, if he fails, at least fails while daring greatly.

~

In a nutshell, the feelings of shame are feelings that we are not enough—not pretty enough, haven't done enough, failed at what we tried to do. The antidote to shame is risking the claim that "I *am* enough"—a step that requires courage in a culture based on scarcity, comparison, and success. Brene's work is really about helping both women and men to let go of the shame they have learned and carry, and that is often very deep in our DNA. She asserts that this involves becoming vulnerable—not with everyone, but with people with whom we can share our feelings of shame. In my awareness of self and others, shame is a major obstacle to the deep wisdom we ask for in the Serenity Prayer.

This resonates in the part of the Serenity Prayer where we are called to discern what to do and with whom to share our lives. It is a challenge to let go of shame in a society that is so shame-based and competitive! In this vein, a story in the beginning of the Hebrew Bible in the Book of Genesis describes the creation of the first human beings. There in the Garden are Adam and Eve. The tempter approaches Eve and says it is okay to eat from the tree of knowledge of good and evil, even though the Creator told them not to do so. Eve eats from the fruit of that tree and persuades Adam to do the same. The infamous story of the fall! Realizing they are naked, they clothe themselves, and Adam blames Eve for suggesting he eat of the fruit. A perfect story about shame and its effects! In the presence of shame, we hide and cover ourselves and usually begin to blame others for what happened. As Brene's research shows, shame is a very powerful impediment to living creatively. I would also add that discovering and trusting the wisdom within us would help us decide and choose what to do here and now.

A second piece related to claiming more intuitive ways of knowing is feeling connected to oneself, others, and Higher Power—the awareness that we are not alone in the universe. There are sources of knowledge and information beyond the naked eye and mind. Be aware that potentially everyone and everything has a lesson to teach us—every being, everything within the universe—can be a teacher for us. Develop an expectation that this is the case; this deep sense of connectedness is at the base of this ability to learn from everyone and everything. Remember the Zen adage: when the student is ready, the teacher shows up. That resonates with keeping our wonder and curiosity alive.

As I have prayed the Serenity Prayer for many years, I have, at times, thought that "Serenity Prayer" is not the best name for this prayer. A more appropriate name would be "Wisdom Prayer"—because, at its core, this prayer is asking for a discerning heart and mind to know the difference between accepting and acting. This is a skill we all need to develop. At times, the answer that comes does not lead to serenity—rather, it can lead to great anxiety and fear about what is coming. I think asking for and developing wisdom—like for Solomon—is really the name of the game of life. We are all in need of wisdom.

Rather than making any other change to the Serenity Prayer—I have only added the line that speaks of being grateful for what we have been given, but the change is substantive. Gratitude is elemental when seeking to live with more happiness. In other words, don't just ask; be sure to say thanks. Adding gratitude to the Serenity Prayer can help us to be grateful for what others have given us in *all* aspects of our life. Prayer and life really do go hand in hand!

Reflection Questions

1.) Who are wise people who have been part of your journey? Practice gratitude in giving thanks for their presence in your life.

2.) What stands in the way of your being more intuitive?

3.) What wisdom has your life and the life of the whole universe taught you? How are you wise?

CONCLUSION

Writing this book felt a little like a recapitulation of my life, especially naming the people who have been sources of wisdom in teaching me about the meaning of life in general as well as the meaning of my own life. I feel wisdom emerging as I look back over these people and the "chance" experiences of my life. I believe something larger than myself, a truly Higher Power, is at work within my life and even in my struggle to write this book..

An image that comes to me as this book concludes is that my life now is like a table. Each of its four legs is important in keeping the table in balance. There is the leg of gratitude, giving thanks for what I have been given; the leg of serenity from learning to accept the things that I cannot change; the leg of courage and risking the choice to change the things I can; and the last leg of wisdom. I continue to be curious and discerning. All of these are elemental, individually and as a whole. They are core aspects of the Serenity Prayer and of recovery as outlined in the Twelve Steps. These are elemental.

I invite you to pray the Serenity Prayer, adding

gratitude and being open to what might emerge for you in saying it in this way. Prayers grow and change as we pray them. Don't be afraid to pray and ask for what is important and vital to you—it might just be given to you and to this world we share.

> May you be serene,
> may you be courageous,
> may you be wise,
> may you be grateful,
> may you be capable of making the changes you wish to make,
> and may you discover a Higher Power that sustains and supports you.
> *Namaste!*

APPENDIX 1
THE TWELVE STEPS

In listing the Twelve Steps, I have phrased them so they can be applied to any addiction issue—alcohol, gambling, sex, drugs, overworking, etc. I chose Higher Power rather than God in the listing of the Steps, because the concept of God turns certain people away from working the Steps and attending Twelve Step groups. The concept of Higher Power is more applicable to the experiences of a wide variety of people.

1. We admitted we were powerless over addictive behavior—that our lives had become unmanageable.

2. We came to believe that a power greater than ourselves could restore us to sanity.

3. We made a decision to turn our will and our lives over to the care of our Higher Power, as we understand our Higher Power.

4. We made a searching and fearless moral inventory of ourselves.

5. We admitted to our Higher Power, to ourselves, and to another human being the exact nature of our wrongs.

6. We were entirely ready to have our Higher Power remove all these defects of character.

7. We humbly asked to have our shortcomings removed.

8. We made a list of all persons we had harmed and became willing to make amends to each of them.

9. We made direct amends to such people wherever possible, except when to do so would injure them or others.

10. We continued to take personal inventory and when we were wrong, promptly admitted it.

11. We sought through prayer and meditation to improve our conscious contact with our Higher Power, praying only for the knowledge of who we are called to be and for the power to carry that out.

12. Having had a spiritual awakening as a result of these Steps, we tried to carry this message to other addicts and to practice these principles in all of our affairs.

APPENDIX 2

BIBLIOGRAPHY & SUGGESTED READING LIST

Alcoholism Guide www.the-alcoholism-guide.org

Alcoholics Anonymous, *Twelve Steps and Twelve Traditions*, AA World Services, Inc., 1952.

Betz, CPCC, Ann and Ursula Pottinga, CPCC, *BEabove Leadership: The Art and Science of Human Transformation*, BEabove Leadership, LLC.

Bingham, June, *Courage to Change: An Introduction to the Life and Thought of Reinhold Niebuhr, Augustus M. Kelley Pubs*, 1972.

Bridges, William, *Making Sense Out of Life's Transitions*, Revised Edition, De Capo Press, 2004.

Brown, Brene, *Daring Greatly: How the Courage to Be Vulnerable Transforms the Way We Live, Love, Parent, and Lead*, Penguin Putnam, Inc., 2012.

Emmons, Robert, *Gratitude Works! A 21-Day Program for Creating Emotional Prosperity*, Jossey-Bass, 2013.

_____. *Thanks! How Practicing Gratitude Can Make You Happier*, Houghton Mifflin, 2008.

Hanh, Thich Nhat, *True Love*, Shambhala, Boston, and London, 2011.

Jung, Carl, *Synchronicity: An Acausal Connecting Principle*, Princeton University Press, 1960.

Kurtz, Ernie, *Not God: A History of Alcoholics Anonymous*, Hazelden, 1991.

Moore, Thomas, *A Religion of One's Own: A Guide to Creating a Personal Spirituality in a Secular World*, Gotham, 2014.

Plato, *Dialogue with Theaetetus*, Hackett Classics, 1990.

Progoff, Ira, The *Cloud of Unknowing: A New Translation of a Classic Guide to Spiritual Experience Revealing the Dynamics of the Inner Life From a Particular Historical and Religious Point of View*, Julian Press, 1957.

_____. *Jung, Synchronicity and Human Destiny*, Dell Delta, 1973.

Random House, *Random House College Dictionary, Revised Edition*, based on the Random House Dictionary of the English Language, Unabridged Edition, 1984.

_____. *Thanks! How Practicing Gratitude Can Make You Happier*, Houghton Mifflin, 2008.

Riesman, David, and Nathan Glazer, *Lonely Crowd: A Study of the American Character*, Revised, Yale University Press, 2001.

Scott, Stuart, *Every Day I Fight*, Blue Rider Press, NY, 2015.

Shaw, George Bernard, *Back to Methuselah: A Metabiological Pentateuch*, Constable and Company, Ltd., 1921.

ACKNOWLEDGMENTS

What would a book on gratitude be without expressing gratitude and thanks to the many folks whose ideas have stimulated my thinking and whose encouragement keeps me going? My sincere thanks to my wife Elaine, who has been a rich source of support over the many years of our relationship and who has taught me many things, among which are the perspective of an artist and a willingness to forgive and move on. I am grateful to two men's groups I have belonged to for many years. One is a small group that has met for thirty years a couple of mornings a month—I am grateful to Joel and Gerry; and John, who died a couple of years ago; and our newest member, Dodd. I thank the members of the Twelve Step group I have belonged to and benefited from for twenty years and from whom I first learned the Serenity Prayer. Their witness and experience have grounded me deeply in the Twelve Steps and in the importance of having a community for recovery.

I am grateful for and to the Dominican community of priests and brothers who supported me in my youth and provided me with an excellent education in philosophy and theology. They opened doors that brought me to places I do not think I would have reached without them. Even though I decided to leave the community and marry, they hold a special place in my heart. A particular person in that community who is a great teacher in theology for me and continues to be a very close friend is Thomas O'Meara.

My thanks to the community of St. Joan of Arc in Minneapolis, where my wife and I have each found a home as well as a community that continues to challenge us to grow and expand our thinking. I thank the many women and men who have taught me so much and extended offers of friendship to me and to us

I thank the people who read this manuscript and offered invaluable comments and suggestions. I especially thank three people who offered detailed comments and critiques: Elaine Gaston, Tom O'Meara, and Ed Sellner. In this, I learned that, in asking for help, there is a need for humility which, as Emmons points out, is an essential aspect of gratefulness and gratitude.

I-thank Marly Cornell, who helped me take lots of ideas about gratitude and the Serenity Prayer and shape them into a more coherent narrative. Thanks also to Marie

Thielen, a long-time friend, colleague, and artist, for her photograph that graces the front cover. I am grateful for the many people whose examples and words of wisdom have helped me immensely.

ABOUT THE AUTHOR

Originally from Chicago, Mark Scannell attended the University of Notre Dame for two years before joining the Dominican community and eventually becoming a Roman Catholic priest in 1969. He left the priesthood fifteen years later, after falling in love with Elaine Gaston, who was a Dominican sister. They married in 1985.

Mark has worked as a consultant, a counselor, a life coach, and a co-owner of a manufacturer's representative's plumbing company. Since retiring from the plumbing business, Mark enjoys officiating weddings, umpiring softball, reading, deepening friendships, cheering for 'Ol Notre Dame, being amazed at the many synchronistic events in his life and in the lives of others, and learning more about the flexibility and plasticity of the human brain. He is in the process of becoming certified as a neurotransformational coach. Mark and Elaine live in Minneapolis, Minnesota, and are members of St. Joan of Arc Catholic Church in Minneapolis.

Please share your insights and feedback with Mark
at
gasscann@bitstream.net
www.thegratitudeelement.com.

Thank you in advance!